Job

The 21st Century Version

By Ralph L. Stephenson

Book is basis
of talk on Rev 3:17

Ralph Stephenson

1

Table of Contents

Forward

The book of Job is perhaps the most enigmatic book in the whole of the Bible. Commentaries on this book give a very wide range of opinions as to its purpose. Presented herewith is a new look at this very old book, which is an attempt to put the plot into a modern setting.

In 1958 a popular play by Archibald MacLeish titled "J. B." was released which I saw when I was a graduate student at the university. The play attempted to put the story in a modern setting for its time, namely the 50's at the height of the cold war. At the end of the play, the actors playing God and Satan were walking off the stage when God says, "See, he was righteous," to which Satan replies, "But he did get his reward," implying that Job was righteous because he was rewarded and thereby Satan was rebutting God.

The book of Job was most undoubtedly written during the Babylonian captivity, is a allegory, and is a lament about God, or more properly, God's failure to help the Jews win their war with the Babylonians and God's allowing the destruction of their country, their temple, and their capital Jerusalem as well as their captivity. The location of the story is vague but is somewhere in the Middle East; and the time is vague too, merely alludes to having taken place a very long time ago. However, assuming it actually was written before the captivity is the same as assuming a Louis Lamour western novel was written in the time setting of the novels plots, namely the 19th century, even though Mr. Lamour wrote his novels near the mid 20th century.

The plot shows God to be very capricious and immature, allowing his pet human, who, like a pet dog, dutifully sits, barks, rolls over, fetches, and does other things to please his master; then God allows Satan to torture his pet, ostensibly to test him to see whether he obeys for rewards or because he believes. God is not depicted in a very good light here, indeed, who is the villain?

So, who is on trial here? Ostensibly of course, it is Job who is being tried, but it is God who defends itself. It is not to subtly suggested that it is not Job who is being tried, rather it is God itself who is actually on trial for allowing such bad things to happen to good people. In the end God has to defend its actions. In the book and in the play in the end Job gets all his physical things back from God, but, of course, he lost most of his original family. This is reminiscent of the Holocaust survivors who lost everything but survived, and then had to remake their lives; so the story is truly a lament about God not doing what humans expected and not defending its people; but it is also a story of survival under difficult circumstances and recovery.

The book is evocative of the story of a group of Rabbis in Auschwitz, who were preparing for Shabbat. As they started they decided to put God on trial for abandoning them to the Nazis. They tried God and found God guilty. Then they resumed preparing for Shabbat services. One doesn't have to read very far between the lines to discover that is what the author of Job is doing surreptitiously, namely, trying God.

Since the book is an allegory, the characters are metaphors. Job is, of course, a metaphor for all humans and the human condition, and his friends are metaphors for the leaders of the world, religious, political, economic, intellectual, etc. The character of God is also somewhat of a metaphor although God appears only briefly to Job and his friends in the original. The content of the book must, like all books of the Bible, be understood within the greater context of the central Biblical themes.

Note that in Hebrew Job's name is Eyob, hence I have named the character E. Job. I have also modernized his friends, namely, the three wise men; Bob Byte, software entrepreneur whose theme is the universe is a computer generating random numbers, Rev. Benjamin Black, minister, who believes in a personal god and that Job has secretly sinned, and Professor Quentin Quantum, an agnostic who says "If God exists why would God care?"

Note that the author is a Mason who believes in "The great architect of the universe" and a religious person who has a deep belief in the existence of God, however, personal experience and historical events, such as the Holocaust and the various historical genocides have convinced him that God does not intervene in human affairs to save large groups of people, but perhaps it does intervene in small ways to help individuals.

The Author

Chapter 1 – Introducing E. Job Goodfellow

Take the case of one E. Job Goodfellow, an honorable and honest man, who is about to experience a most unusual and unpleasant adventure, one he will wish he never had.

E. Job had lived a good life. He owned a number of factories that produced the disks and instructions for software and boxed them for use on personal and business computers. He did this as a subcontractor for the software companies that developed the programs. He had become a billionaire and gave huge amounts to charities to help the sick and the poor and gave his employees a share of the business, allowing them to share in the profits.

He had married a beauty queen early in life shortly after he started his first factory. The couple had four children, two boys and two girls. E. Job gave as much time as he could to raising his children but business and charitable work were always demanding of his time; he regretted not being able get his progeny to appreciate the morals and ethics that drove him. Upon graduation he gave each child $20 million to start their own business.

One of the boys stated a payroll lending business, which cashed checks for poor people for an exorbitant fee and loaned them money, also at interest rates much above bank and credit union rates. It was a very profitable business but oppressed poor people who really couldn't afford the service but were forced to use it because they could not get the service elsewhere. The service was especially harsh on illegal aliens who had difficulty doing business in normal ways. Although not illegal, it was certainly unethical.

The other boy set up a bank in a banana republic and accepted deposits in cash from shady characters, as well as people who wished to hide their profits from tax collectors. The bank was very private, and maintained its privacy by giving huge cash bribes to the officials of the banana republic in which it was located. The deposits were then recycled into various legal enterprises; essentially a money laundering bank for criminals. It was an extremely profitable business, and of questionable legality as well as being unethical.

The sisters had married lawyers whose specialty was to take firms private, paying shareholders almost nothing, and then selling off all the profitable assets, taking the proceeds for themselves and leaving the shareholders bankrupt. While perfectly legal it was most certainly unethical.

E. Job could see that his progeny were not following in his footsteps and fasted and offered prayers for them. He also attempted to help those his sons were oppressing by setting up clinics and aid stations in the barrios and other places where poor people lived.

Chapter 2 – The Grand Council of the Universe

After God had created the universe and it expanded to unimaginable size, sentient life began to appear on billions of planets. God knew everything but soon the cacophony of information generated by all these sentient species became too much to bear and God created ten thousand archangels, each of which managed a section of the universe.

Every few million years God would call Grand Council of all the Archangels and have them report what was happening in their sectors.

At such a council God asked Lucifer, "How goes it in the 314th sector?"

"Well," said Lucifer, "many of the sentient's are warring with one another, contrary to your precepts." Lucifer was an ambitious and crafty being and liked to put other beings on the spot.

God sighed, "Yes, I know, when sentient's get started doing war they never seem to stop, despite the fact I have put it into the philosophy of all sentient species that they must treat each other well."

"Ah yes, how altruistic that is" Lucifer replied sarcastically, "however, I have an interesting case for you. On an exceedingly minute speck of dust called Earth in a small galaxy called the Milky Way is a sentient called E. Job Goodfellow, who obeys your precepts to the letter. Indeed, I have never observed one so compliant with your philosophy, morals, and ethics. But, everything he does profits him as you have decreed. Remove these blessings and he will curse you to your face and behave like all the other sentient's."

"So," observed God, "you are saying that my precepts are followed only by those who profit from them, therefore the precepts are inefficacious in any other setting."

"Right," noted Lucifer, "let me test this sentient by removing his blessings and he will, like most other sentient's, curse you, or, more likely, ignore you and stop following your rules."

"Hmm," thought God, "so you want to test whether a sentient will follow these precepts because they help everyone or simply because they profit from them."

Lucifer smiled, "Exactly, either your precepts are good to follow under all circumstances or they aren't needed."

"I wouldn't put it in those terms but I don't know, makes me seem capricious and immature if we do this." wavered God.

"So, what's one sentient; there are trillions and trillions of them in the universe, and billions die every day of war, disease, famine, and other causes, mostly brought on by themselves," reasoned Lucifer.

God sighed again, "very well, remove all he has but do not touch his body. Then we will see."

Lucifer left smiling.

Chapter 3 – The Beginning

E. Job was sitting at his desk in the office tower that he leased when his contracts administrator called and said, "I have to see you immediately."

"Come on up." replied E. Job.

The contracts administrator rushed into his office and exclaimed, "All your contracts with all the software companies have been cancelled!"

"What, all of them! How is that possible?" exclaimed E. Job.

"Easy, an Asian company offered to make the packages at half the price we were charging. Every software company called within minutes of each other and cancelled the contract immediately. We are to ship what is finished, but they don't even want what is on the assembly lines," exclaimed the very agitated man.

"How can they do that? We would lose money if we matched their price! That means we must close the factories immediately and lay off all the workers." moaned E. Job as he pushed the button to summon his accountant.

The accountant entered and E. Job asked, "You have heard that all factories must be closed now and we must lay off all the workers. I wish to give all a weeks pay for each year of service. What will that cost?"

The accountant pulled out his laptop and fingered a few keys and said, "It will leave you bankrupt. You will have nothing. You don't have to do that you know; there is no legal requirement to do that."

"No," sighed E. Job, "I do have to do that; it's the right thing to do. Please make it so. I appreciate your service and am sad that it must end this way, but perhaps someday in the future things will get better."

"I surely hope so; you have been a wonderful employer," said the accountant and the contracts administrator seconded the sentiment. Both had been with the company for 20 years and would receive a very generous settlement.

E. Job was sitting at his desk in a deep funk, getting ready to box up his belongings when the phone rang.

He picked it up and heard a voice on the other end, "Are you Mr. E. Job Goodfellow?"

"Yes I am."

"I'm Officer Reaper of the sheriff's office. There has been a tornado, which has completely demolished your son's new mansion. We have recovered the bodies of your sons and daughters and their spouses and children. Apparently they were having a housewarming party when it happened. Very sorry to tell you this, sir."

E. Jobs whole body trembled as he said, "Thank you Officer," and hung up the phone.

He boxed his personal belongings up and drove home in his leased Lincoln Continental, but there were several Constable's Patrol cars parked in his driveway. As he got out of the car an officer he knew strode up to him, waving a paper, and said, "Sorry sir, this is an repossession and eviction notice, you and your wife have to move out today. Also we are repossessing the car."

E. Job looked in the garage and noticed his old Honda Civic, which he had never traded in, and asked, "Is that car mine?"

The Officer looked at his list and said, "Not on the list, it's yours."

E. Job's wife came storming down the porch stairs and screamed at him, "What is going on? All the credit cards have been cancelled and the Bank called and said all our assets have been frozen and will be seized by creditors."

"E. Job collapsed on the stairs and said softly, "Everything, ...everything, ...is gone, money, children, everything. The kids and their families were killed this morning; guess you didn't get the news. Factories gone too, Asian company took the business. We have nothing!!"

His wife screamed and sobbed, then screamed and sobbed some more. Finally she calmed down enough to ask, "What are we going to do?"

E. Job was sobbing too but finally pulled himself together and said, "We need to pack our essential clothes and a few other things such as photo albums into the Honda. We will drive it to the shack we bought with cash years ago and still own on the Lake of the Ozarks and think about what to do next when we get there."

On the way there his wife alternated between sobbing and being critical. She repeatedly said, "Where is this God you think so highly of, why did he abandon us? Why didn't he protect our children?"

E. Job answered, "God is God and does what he will. His ways are far above our ways so there must be some purpose in what is happening."

"Well damn it," his wife shot back, "our children weren't moral and ethical like you and still got rich, so how is this God of yours helping? People get rich or stay poor no matter what! And if you say they are dead again and imply that they died because they had no ethics or morals I will start screaming; sure they weren't perfect but neither is anybody else, so why kill them?"

E. Job had no answer so drive on in silence. He had $500 in his pocket when he left, the only money left to him, and they bought gas and groceries with most of it.

Soon they arrived at their old fishing shack on the Lake of the Ozarks. It was a small four room ramshackle building that had little maintenance for years; they had planned on tearing it down and building a retirement home on the lot. It had a leaky roof, no insulation in the walls, electric stove and hot water heater, an old small refrigerator, a fireplace for heat, and a well for water and a septic tank for sewage. It had a porch that looked out over the lake and a decrepit and rotting dock on the lake that once had boats tied up to it. Between the porch and the dock was a large fire pit.

After unpacking, E. Job took his old fishing tackle and went to the dock to fish the rest of the day but caught no fish. That evening he built a large fire in the fire pit. All these activities were to keep away from his wife, who was spitting venom, and to meditate on what had happened.

For weeks E. Job wandered in the woods or fished, avoiding his wife and pondering his fate. He talked to the trees, the birds, the animals, and the wind, asking questions and receiving no answer. "Why, why, why," he would ask himself over and over and never received a reply.

He thought, *Is God punishing me for my children's evil ways? Is there no reward for being good? Why does God do evil by letting me be punished in this way? Is God both good and evil? Why be good when there is no reward? Have I committed some sin unknowingly that I'm being punished for? If I did, why no warning? Why doesn't God answer? Why doesn't God help the righteous, the oppressed, the poor, the sick, the widow, the orphan, and all those who are evilly used? Why doesn't God intervene and correct the ills of society? Why have rules if no one obeys them, rather everyone tries to take advantage of their fellow humans and gets away with it? Indeed, why are they rewarded for doing evil? Why are the good punished for doing good?*

E. Job paused and tried to meditate, realized that the questions he was asking were general, then thought some more concerning himself and others, *"Why was I born? What is the meaning of life? Why is anyone or I living and breathing?   Hmm, is there really an afterlife? Indeed, is there really a god?*

Chapter 4 – The Interlude and Phase Two

After a few weeks Satan requested an audience with God. God granted the request.

"Well Lucifer," God greeted Satan, "How goes the E. Job trial."

Lucifer sneered, "The guys a bleeding nut case. He just wanders around in a daze trying to understand the unfathomable."

"I notice that you did not touch his wife, but I gave you permission to do what you wish to all his family. Why didn't you kill her along with the children?" asked God

"Oh her," countered Lucifer, "she's a damn bitch, a first class gold-digger and back stabber! She's one nabob of negativism. Why kill her, she's on my side?"

"Hmm," mused God, "probably the reason the kids didn't turn out to well don't you think?"

"Maybe partially," replied Lucifer, "but some of the blame has to be assigned to your pet; he should have spent more time with them."

"Perhaps, but everyone is responsible for their own actions. He did do what he could so I can't fault him on that. So what now?" asked God.

"Simple, let me touch his body so he is in excruciating pain and he will break. No sentient can stand torture." replied Lucifer, licking his chops at the prospect.

"Some do and some don't break under torture, a fact. But, OK, let's take it to the last level and see what happens, we've gone this far, might as well complete the cycle." sighed God, who was already sorry he had agreed to this despite the good results so far.

Lucifer wasted no time in causing E. Job to contract a virulent form of military grade Smallpox. E. Job broke out all over his skin in tiny pustules of water, which caused unbearable itching; and he experienced fever as well as excruciating pain in his bowels and his bones. He could not wear clothes as they irritated his skin; rather he wore only an old but soft pair of shorts. Soon he climbed onto the pile of ashes in the fire pit, which were soft and acted as a salve, which drew out the water from the pustules. He moaned and groaned with pain day and night.

His wife complained bitterly, "I can't sleep with all that moaning and groaning. Why don't you just curse that stupid mean God you serve, maybe he'll be merciful and kill you? In your condition you'd be better off dead anyway, don't you think?"

E. Job could do nothing but moan and groan. He had to concede that she was right about one thing; he wished he could die so the pain would stop.

Chapter 5 – The Friends

E. Job's horrible experience made the news briefly then he faded into the background. He had had his 15 seconds of unwanted fame and everyone forgot him except three of his friends. They came to visit him.

The first friend was Bob Byte, a software entrepreneur who had given E. Job his first contract to produce boxes of his software. Bob had started his business in his garage and became a billionaire, but he was good hearted, a free spirit, and somewhat of a 60's style Hippie.

The second was Rev. Benjamin Black, pastor of a mega-church and E. Job's clergyman. He was a popular theologian of some note who had written several books on how to be a good Christian and had a TV show. He preached the popular health-wealth pull yourself up by your own bootstraps doctrine and believed in a personal god that helped his worshipers. He was also a conservative evangelical.

The third was Professor Quentin Quantum, an astronomer and Astro-physicist who served on several of the boards of the charities E. Job had set up.   He had also written several textbooks and was called by reporters "the smartest man in the room." He was a very moral and upright man who believed, like E. Job, that humans should help their fellows and should help maintain the planet.   However, although he had a Jewish upbringing, he was somewhat of an agnostic.

They arrived and E. Job's wife provided old lawn chairs for them to sit in front of E. Job. They were astounded at his condition and couldn't think of anything to say for almost an hour; they just sat there thinking and nodded or shook their heads in amazement.

Suddenly, E. Job looked up and recognized them.   "Wow, I didn't think anyone cared, thank you for coming, but I'm sorry you have to see me in this state; I believe that God may have done this, or at least allowed it to happen, but I don't understand why."

Bob fumbled in his pocket and pulled out a package of joints. He offered one to E. Job, but he declined, then he offered one to each of the others but they declined as well. He lit up and said, while exhaling a cloud of fragrant smoke, "Hey man, you ought to try one of these, it'll help ease the pain and make you feel better. After all, God made this stuff for us to use didn't he? Anyway, the universe is all ones and O's, that is, it's like a computer spewing out random numbers. Sometimes these numbers line up and life forms. Sometimes you hit a string of luck and sometimes you hit a string of jinxes; it's all karma man. For a long time you had good karma and now you have bad karma. Loosen up and take one of these joints, at least you'll feel better; give you better karma. And maybe the numbers will realign and your string of luck will return, who knows. It's all random, man, we don't control it."

E. Job sat there for a while contemplating what his friend Bob had said, then replied, "No, you're saying there is no God, and the universe is a giant computer that operates on random numbers. There has to be a God, after all, who created the universe; but why is there so much evil. Did God create evil?"

Bob chuckled and said, "Cool it man, so who made God? If everyone would chill out we could eliminate a lot of evil."

Rev. Ben interrupted, "I disagree. I firmly believe that there is a God who takes a personal interest in us, and who rules the universe. No, E. Job has committed some great sin and brought this upon himself. He must repent and seek God's forgiveness; and if he does then perhaps God will restore his health and wealth. Evil is of Men and good is of God."

Bob chuckled again, "Yeah right, so disease, which is evil, is of men? No way, those microbes were here long before us. When we happened along they found us good eating and started chomping away. Now war and poverty and pollution I agree is of men; so we have a mixed bag here, but still, random numbers man, …random numbers."

E. Job said in a hoarse voice, "But you are denying God exists and that is not possible!"

Bob threw up his hands and said, "Hey, let the dominos fall where they may! If God exists he is doing a hell of a job screwing things up for us humans. Yep, he could help but seems to not care, or perhaps he doesn't exist. I believe the latter is more logical. Indeed, I suggest that it is more possible that God does not exist than that he does. You're kind of living proof of that."

Rev. Ben interrupted again, "We're missing the point here. We need to find what great sin E. Job has committed and bring him to repentance." Turning to E. Job, " What is your sin my good man?"

E. Job groaned and said, "The only thing I can think of is my children lost their way and did some very bad things."

"Ah yes!" exclaimed Rev. Bob, "there we have it. God visits the sins to the third and fourth generations. Hallelujah, God be praised E. Job, you only need to repent of not raising your children right and God will forgive you; you can be blest once more!"

"Wait, hold it bible thumper!" exclaimed Bob, "I may not have a great respect of or belief in God but as it happens I do know what the Bible says and what it says is 'the sins of the fathers will be visited on the children to the third and fourth generations.' Now it goes down, not up, and his kids were killed so that would be the end of the matter. No man, it's random numbers...random numbers."

E. Jobs wife was bringing cold water to her guests and happened to overhear that part of the conversation, "Damn you, Rev. Bob, we raised our children the best we could and they turned out no better and no worse than any others so I don't see how you can judge us on that; besides I understand you son is gay and your daughter sleeps around which you disapprove of so how are our kids worse than yours in your eyes? You're a hypocrite! Why isn't God punishing you if you think that way?" She then handed each a glass of cold water, said, "sorry, water is all we have to give you," and angrily stomped back to the house.

"Man," exclaimed Bob, "that is one hell of an angry woman. How do you live with her?"

E. Job chuckled for the first time in many weeks, "I don't, I live out here and she lives in there. She wants me to curse God and die; and I must admit dying sounds good right now but I will not curse God."

Bob chuckled, "cursing something that doesn't exist is a fruitless exercise. If you want to die I can get you some good stuff that will let you go very happy."

A horrified Rev. Bob exclaimed, "but you will wind up in hell if you do that! This man is tempting you, resist temptation E. Job, call on the almighty to help you and forgive your sins and you will be washed white as snow."

Bob looked at Rev. Ben and shook his head, "Damn, you're really full of bullshit aren't you; you really need one of these joints, I understand your daughter uses them all the time and I'm told by those that know that she's a real tiger in bed."

Bob's intentional jab at the Rev. made Ben red-faced and angry, but he controlled his anger and spat out, "Get thee behind me Satan!"

Professor Quentin spoke for the first time, "Wait a minute fellows, aren't we getting a little off base here. I have served on many of E. Job's charities and know him to be a good and righteous man who cares for his fellow man, and contributes immense amounts of his time and money to good causes that benefit the poor and the Earth. If he did commit some sin I'm sure it has been offset many times over by all the good he has done, so let's forget the secret sin crap!"

"Yeah," replied Bob, "I see that too."

Rev. Ben sat in a funk and said nothing. Nearly thirty minutes passed, no one saying anything, then E. Jobs wife came out to collect the glasses, gave a sharp look at E. Job and said vehemently, "Curse God you idiot." She then carried the glasses back into the shack.

Bob chuckled and asked, "How the hell did you wind up marrying her anyway. That stare of hers could turn hot water into ice."

E. Job chuckled once again between moans, "She has her good points, and is a good mother despite all that seemed wrong with out kids. Everyone makes their own choices and must answer for them."

Rev Ben suddenly had an idea and exclaimed, "I've got it! E. Job's sin is self-righteousness! Repent and God will forgive you!"

"You're right Bob," replied Professor Quantum, "Ben is full of Bullshit! Damn Ben, I serve on the boards of nearly all of E. Job's charities, and not a single one is named after himself or his companies. I can attest that there is no humbler man in existence, indeed, he makes all donations as anonymously as he can, so no, there is no way he is self-righteous.

A somewhat shaken and irritated Rev. Ben turned to Quentin and asked, "Indeed! OK Professor, what is your answer?"

Quentin shook his head and said, "Actually, I have none, or at least, no definitive answers. However, consider this, the universe is fantastically immense. The Earth and the entire solar system is not even a speck of dust compared to the Milky Way galaxy, and the entire galaxy with its trillions of stars is not even a speck of dust in the immensity of the universe and its trillions of galaxies. In these galaxies are trillions and trillions of planets many of which probably sustain life, and many of which, maybe billions, which probably have sentient beings such as us on them."

"Mind blowing," said Bob as he took another puff on his joint.

"Yes, but there is more," continued Quentin, "Quantum Theory indicates that there are nine physical dimensions, of which we occupy only three, time is not a physical dimension but is a dimension. Unified field theory requires 47 dimensions to work and again we only occupy four dimensions, including time. So what are in those other dimensions? We don't know. Therefore I cannot say for certainty that there is a God or there isn't. But, if there is a God of the Universe, why should he, she, or it take any interest whatsoever in anything that goes on in this incredibly minute speck of dust called Earth? In a sense Bob is right. If there is a God of the Universe we are not even the unnoticeable microbes on a speck of sand that is under the feet of someone strolling along a beach."

"Way, Way out Man," mumbled Bob as he slumped down in his lawn chair.

Rev. Bob interjected, "Surely, even if what you say is true there has to be a God who takes a personal interest in us. Isn't God infinite and therefore able to know about us even in the vast expanse of the Universe?"

E. Job moaned again and redistributed his weight on the ashes, "Thank you my friends but your answers seem to be that either there is no God and I have simply fallen on bad times, or there is a God who is punishing me for some sin. No, I believe there is a God and God is testing me, but I don't know why. So what are the answers to the big questions of life such as; why do bad things happen to good people? Why were we born? What is the purpose of life? What is the meaning of life? And dozens of other like questions. What are the answers? Where are the answers? Who has these elusive answers?"

It was late in the afternoon and Bob perked up and exclaimed, "Hey, I haven't eaten since breakfast and I'm hungry, anyone else hungry?" All answered in the affirmative so Bob pulled out his phone and ordered BBQ meals from a restaurant down the road to be delivered.

The meals came in about thirty minutes and all started eating. Even E. Job ate some BBQ, he hadn't eaten much for weeks, was feeling better in the company of friends, and commented on how good it was.

Chapter 6 – God Answers

It was late that evening, about dusk, when a small tornado appeared from the South and stopped over the boat dock without harming it. A man appeared out of the tornado, which then disappeared. The man was average height, build, and had an average face. If one saw him in a crowd they would immediately forget him. He started walking along the dock toward the path to the fire pit.

E. Job awoke from his food induced sleep at the sound of the tornado and shouted to the man, "Careful, there's rotten boards on that dock that won't support you!"

The man continued walking toward them, appearing and disappearing like a mirage' but his feet seemed to be a few inches above the ground. He reached the fire pit circle and sat down on a lawn chair that magically appeared.

"Who are you?" asked everyone almost simultaneously.

"I'm God," said the man in a low voice, "I heard you talking about me so I decided to join the conversation and set the record straight."

"Wow, E. Job," exclaimed Bob, "I heard you had a company experimenting with CGI but this is fantastic. It's holographic and everything; better then anything my people or I could do. So this was all a setup to demonstrate your new holographic CGI right?"

"Sorry Bob, I don't have such a company, this man probably really is God," replied E. Job.

Quentin asked the man, "How do I know that you're God and not some hallucination or, like Bob says, a CGI or some other trick?"

Rev. Ben sat dumbfounded.

"Humpff," retorted the man who claimed to be God, "What proof do you want that I am God?"

"I donno," said Bob, " maybe do a miracle?"

Rev. Ben finally screwed up his courage and asked, "How do we know that you are not an evil spirit?"

Quentin sat, thinking and observing.

"Hmm, OK," said God, "I'm going to give each of you a hallucination of something you want and have dreamed about." He waved his hands for dramatic effect.

Bob found himself on a beach in the South Seas looking at a group of native young women swimming in the ocean in the nude. They were beckoning him to come in.

Rev. Ben found himself at the Pearly Gates talking to St. Peter, who said, "come in and enjoy paradise you good and faithful servant."

Quentin found himself looking down on the Milky Way Galaxy with hundreds of equations running through his brain. He suddenly understood many things.

E. Job saw himself and his wife being married, then bringing the children home one by one from the Hospital.

All of a sudden they all snapped out of their reveries and found themselves in Missouri at the Lake again.

"Convinced?" asked God.

"Really cool," exclaimed Bob, "best hallucination ever, what drug did you give us?"

Rev. Ben asked, "Evil Spirits can probably do that as well, how do we know you aren't of the evil kind."

God answered, "No drugs, I merely facilitated converting the desires of your minds into those hallucinations. As far as being evil, you will have to judge by what I will tell you. But the visions prove something, convinced now?" He paused but no one spoke, "OK, I see you still have doubts but let's get down to it shall we?" "

"Hey man," said Bob, "I really would have liked to finish that one!"

"Fine," said God, "but we have other things to do right now. Let's see, the first question is why do bad things happen to good people, right? Well, that's one of the easy ones, the simple answer being usually because bad people do bad things to good people, but it goes further than that; sure as the bumper stickers say, 'Shit Happens' and random things occur, but most of the bad things that happen you do to yourselves. Why blame me for genocides and wars; you do that to yourselves? I had nothing to do with it! You build houses in flood plains and when it floods and damages the houses you call it an 'act of god'. Why! You know it floods there yet you ignore the obvious?"

Rev. Ben was getting up his courage now and asked, "but what about lightning, forest fires volcano eruptions, tsunamis, and so forth?"

God rolled his eyes, "These are all natural events that obey the laws of nature. Lightning kills but you use the same laws to light your houses, power your appliances, and so forth. Yes, nature is somewhat random but as you understand it you can prevent, or at least mitigate these bad things from happening. It is your responsibility to take care of your planet and to understand it, not mine!"

"But what about those terrible storms and changing climate, why don't you do something?" queried Rev. Ben?

God chuckled, then said in an increasing volume, "You pollute your air and complain about how hard it is to breath, and you pollute your water and complain about all the diseases you get from it. You are steadily generating climate change by polluting your air, which will ultimately destroy your planet.

You have the super rich who give nothing to the poor so you have both poverty and a high crime rate; what choice have you given them? Almost everyone owns a gun yet you complain about crime and how criminals always seem to have guns; and the list goes on and on. YOU are responsible for these things, and YOU caused them, NOT ME! It is YOUR responsibility to fix them, NOT MINE!"

"Fine," said Rev. Ben, screwing up his courage after being hammered on by God, "But how about E. Job here?"

Instantaneously God changed from an man to a woman with the same height and facial looks, but now had a dress and feminine body form and said in a feminine, but authoritative version of the male voice, "Ah, well, E. Job is a good man and received the rewards good men should get but frequently don't." explained the now female God, "When I created the universe I established precepts to govern sentient life and instilled in the societies of these sentient's these precepts; and you should know there are billions of planets with sentient life. Unfortunately many species get started by becoming tribalistic and warring on each other and tend to forget these precepts. This behavior usually eventually results in the extinction of all life on their planet, either by nuclear annihilation or climate change caused by pollution. About 5% of the planets inhabited by sentient's have already ended that way."

"So, what are these precepts and how do they work?" asked Bob.

"Simple, really," the Goddess replied, "in fact if you read any of your holy books you would find them embedded there along with a lot of crap put there by idiots. They are, 'Treat your fellow sentient's like you would like to be treated and take care of your home, that is, your planet;' after all why trash your home, which is what you're are doing by the way."

"Wait a minute," shouted Rev. Ben; "you forgot 'love God with all your heart' didn't you."

"No, but if it helps you can do that, but it means nothing to me whether you love me or not, you better think about the ones next to you though." The Goddess replied matter of factly. Then added, "I didn't even know you existed until recently and we wouldn't be talking right now except a certain archangel sucked me into a situation; so no, I don't care one way or the other."

"Can I ask a question?" said Rev. Ben.

"Sure."

Rev. Ben asked timidly, "why have you changed from a man to a woman?

The Goddess chuckled, "I'm neither male nor female: I am the Supreme Being; I have no sex or am all sexes, take your choice."

"Hmm," vocalized Rev. Ben, itching with curiosity, "What is the afterlife like?"

"Why do you think there is an afterlife?" replied the Goddess.

"Because the Bible tells me there is one!" exclaimed the Rev.

The Goddess chuckled, "Your Bible and all holy books are very contradictory. In fact, humans wrote them, and although they usually contain my precepts the human writers added a lot of stupidity with nefarious objectives in mind, like getting people to obey them with the promise of an afterlife. But, I'm not going to answer the question about an afterlife because if you do good things in order to have a good afterlife then you are doing them for the wrong reason; you should do good things because they help your fellow humans. Perhaps doing good for the wrong reason is better than not doing good at all, but in the end it will bite you because doing good for a reward rather than to help your fellows is selfish and will gain the reward of the selfish. But I'll give you a hint, there are actually 47 dimensions as needed by the Unified Field Equation."

"I don't understand," wailed Rev. Ben.

"Unfortunately, I doubt you will ever understand, however, Quentin here will probably understand in time if he doesn't already." answered the Goddess.

E. Job listened with interest, and then asked, "What is the meaning of life? Why are we here and why were we born?"

The Goddess smiled, "Ah, better questions now; you're purpose is to learn and then to pass on what you learned to the next generation, and so on, until you know how to live in peace with one another and how to maintain your home, your planet. If you don't achieve that you will all die by your own hand. Note that you, like all sentient species, determine your own fate. Interestingly, about 5% of sentient species have achieved a sustainable life and live in peace, so it can be done. I have allowed all sentient beings to evolve to the point where they achieve intellect and have free choice; but free choice carries the responsibility to choose wisely. So please choose life and peace."

Professor Quantum was curious and asked, "Why did you create the universe?"

The Goddess chuckled again, "Oh, I don't know, seemed like a good thing to do at the time and it's been enjoyable seeing everything moving all these billions of years."

Professor Quantum spoke again, "Pardon me, but where did you come from; who created you?"

Goddess looked serious and replied, "Ah yes, the great mystery? I am that I am. You just have to accept that. It was I that initiated the singularity that blew up to create the universe. It was I who decreed that the universe would conform to the Unified Field Equation with 47 dimensions. It is I who inhabit the vast expanse of the Universe. Physical boundaries or the 47 dimensions or time does not limit me. I am that I am!"

E. Job asked, "What will become of me?"

Goddess looked very sad and said, "You'll find that out when it happens. Unfortunately, right now your species will be extinct in less than 200 years unless you change your ways drastically and soon. It is a race to see if extinction will come by nuclear annihilation or by climate change. The population of this planet is already far beyond a sustainable number and you profligately consume your resources polluting your air with all kinds of noxious chemicals, particularly carbon dioxide which is causing rapid warming of your planet. No, you have, maybe at most, 200 years right now."

"Sorry, that was informative and interesting,... and uh, frightening, " said E. Job, "but I meant me personally."

"Oh!" exclaimed Goddess, "Sorry, I always think in terms of the big picture. I ask that your friends here give you resources so you can rebuild your life; your trial is about at an end. To Bob I say discover real spirituality, I know you have it in you; to Rev. Ben I recommend you warn people about their real sins, namely overpopulation and excessive consumption, urge them to live sustainably; and to Quentin, I recommend that you continue your studies and continue to help E. Job; you are indeed 'the smartest man in the room' and are very close to the ultimate truth."

There was silence for about half an hour then Goddess proclaimed in a loud voice, "I have given all sentient's the knowledge of good and evil. You have, both individually and collectively, free will and free choice, but you will reap the results of those choices; choose good and good things will happened, but make bad choices and bad things will happen, it is up to you!" She then snapped her fingers.

Everyone woke up to see the sun rising over the lake in the East.

Chapter 7 – Epilog

After they woke up they realized they either dreamed or hallucinated their conversations with God and the Goddess, or did they? They weren't quite certain; it seemed so real and they vividly remembered everything that was said exactly as it was said in their discourse with God.

E. Job however, soon noticed that his fever was gone and his pustules were receding and he no longer itched or was in pain. In fact, he felt quite good so he got up and took a shower to wash the ashes off, put on his clothes, and ate a hearty breakfast.

His wife noticed his recovery and commented, "I'm glad you feel better and hope things get better for us. I'm sorry for the mean things I said and apologize; but I am grieving for our children and am not always feeling good myself. By the way, there are some envelopes for you that your friends left; they said something about God telling them to do it."

E. Job opened the envelopes and there was a check for $500,000 from Bob, a check for $10,000 from Professor Quantum, and a check for $5,000 from Rev. Ben.

E. Job took the money and invested it and became richer than before. He and his wife adopted four special needs children and raised them to adulthood, enabling them to function and survive and succeed as adults. He contributed time and money to many charities as well as causes that tried to reverse climate change.

Bob Byte traveled extensively in Asia and studied many religions. He eventually retired to a Zen Buddhist Monastery in California. He donated his entire fortune of five billion dollars to E. Job's charities.

Rev. Ben continued to preach the health wealth doctrine and a judgmental form of Protestantism. He and his wife were shot and killed by a deranged parishioner who had gone bankrupt; the gun used was legally purchased. The killer claimed he had done everything Rev. Ben told him to do and still failed. At his trial he claimed Rev. Ben was a "false prophet."

Quentin continued his research and ultimately discovered new facets of the Unified Field Theory as well as developing new theories and formulas in the field of Astro-physics.

Unfortunately, humankind did not fare so well. Humans continued to procreate excessively and to squander resources. Wars for increasingly rare resources became more and more violent and cruel. In the meantime the earth was becoming hotter and hotter; deserts were expanding and in other areas intense storms prevented human activity. In 150 years the earth was so hot that humans could no longer exist. The last humans died in a cave in Antarctica in 2177 of starvation and heat stroke.

Lucifer asked for another appointment with God, which God granted.

"Well Lucifer," said God happily, "the experiment was a success, wasn't it. E. Job stayed righteous even in his trials."

"Oh, really," Lucifer spouted sarcastically, "but he did get his reward, didn't he!"

The End

Authors Information

Ralph L. Stephenson, BS, MS, PE, is a professional environmentalist who is retired from his former position as the Environmental Manager of a multi-billion dollar engineering and construction company with worldwide operations and projects.

He is an avid collector of Judiaca, especially coins of the Second Temple era (about 450 BCE to 77 ACE), and is a student of the Bible and Biblical History. He previously authored several books on Biblical history and commentary.

As an Environmental Professional he has traveled extensively and managed environmental issues for projects in dozens of countries. He is an internationally recognized expert in environmental science and technology, and is presently writing both non-fiction books and science fiction novels with the theme of climate change. These visionary novels give scientifically based projections of the effects of climate change and the configuration of the coming post-climate change world.

He has written twelve non-fiction works. Two are a graduate level engineering textbook and a book about the Bible, money and economics. All books are available on Amazon.com, Kindle.com, Createspace.com, and from the author. The five science fiction novels currently available are:

1.   The Confederation Galactica
2.   Toy Boy and the Astrologer
3.   The Second Expedition
4.   The Tentacles of Time
5.   Nothing is What it Seems
6.   A Matter of Survival, coming in 2017

Non-Fiction works of general interest currently available are:

1.   My Family – Plunkett, Clore, Steele, and Stephenson. A history of my family, homesteading, and Kansas.
2.   Publish Free!!!. How to publish your work on Amazon's Createspace

and Kindle for free.

3.   Biblical Living. A book about what the Bible says about how to live our lives.

4.   Home Bartending Made Simple. How to stock a home bar and make mixed drinks.

5.   Common Sense Gun Control. The middle ground for gun control with common sense proposals to keep guns out of the hands of those who misuse them.

6.   Common Sense Doomsday Prepping. How to prepare for the Apocalypse.

7.   Sell it on the Internet. Turn trash to cash by selling on the Internet.

8.   Memoirs of the Second Gulf War, or How the plan to reelect a President destabilized the Middle East

9.   The Seven Religions of the Bible

10.   Job, The 21st Century Version

11.   The Coming Climate Cataclysm,

Coming in 2018.